EXPERIENCES WITH LOVE

AUTHOR

ARNIKIA ROBINSON

ARNIKIA ROBINSON

ISBN-9780988788312

DEDICATION

First, I want to give thanks God who is the ruler and head of my life. For it's through him that all things are possible. If he decides not to do anything else for me in this lifetime, HE'S ALREADY DONE ENOUGH!! Next, I want to dedicate my first poem book to the one's that I have given life to (my children) and my granddaughter. Cree, Vonte, Sammie Lee, and Ar'Nyjah. Even though I gave them life; in return they has given me life (if you can catch that). Thirdly, comes my mother and father; step mother and step father. Each and every one of you has played a role in shaping me into being the woman that I am today. I love you guys. Special shout out to my mother Kathy, for you have showed me the most positive things in life, and that's how to call upon God and be a great mother. I look at you as a role model; I study your footsteps, and try to copy it exactly how you do it i appreciate all your prayers, I appreciate you. Last but not least, I want to say thank you to my siblings, my nieces, and my nephews. I love you guys to death. Tammy and Ashunte, we've been through some things but we never let them break us; because our priority is to always stick together as a family. To the rest of my family and friends, thanks for all the positive and constructive criticism that may have been given to me. Nothing like having; a close- knit family, my cousin Trina Clarke for your help My best friends, and even close friends. Special shout out to my aunt Lillie for inspiring me to do my first book and always being an inspiration in my life!!!!!!!!!

CONTENTS

ARNIKIA ROBINSON

EXPERIENCES WITH LOVE

ARNIKIA ROBINSON

INSPIRATION SECTION first FIVE PAGES

Inspired

I'm inspired
For who I am and loving me
I'm inspired
By the urge and drive of my inner being
I'm inspired
By having Faith, which means
Substance of things hoped for
Evidence of things not seen
Sort of like the fresh air
That our lungs are breathing
I'm inspired
By loving parents
I'm inspired
And having two God- fearing family's
I'm inspired
For the love I have for my three children
I thank the Lord for seeing it fit
To bless me with them
It taught me patience, high tolerance, and perseverance
Through them I experienced
Love beyond the love
That I measure myself with
I'm inspired
By my grandchild So special to me
New found joy of a life worth living
Another chance to make right the area's I failed in
I'm inspired
By my burdens That broke me down

So that God can build me up
A lot stronger
I'm inspired
By the many tears I shed
Because it was once said
"Tears are liquid prayers"
And God never skipped a beat in answering them
I'm inspired
By the protection that covers me
Gliding...
Through dangers seen and unseen
Oh the blood of Jesus is so powering
I'm inspired
By my bestie who was always there
Although she's gone I still feel her presence near
Thanks to you for teaching me the definition of true friendship
I haven't found anyone to fill your void since you left
I'm inspired
For ever challenge that I defeat
Every task that I conquer and complete
Finishing school and earning many degree's
I'm inspired
By those who never gave up on me
I'm inspired
By my struggles because they kept me striving
For my heart aches and head aches
For making me a tougher woman

My Blessings

Someone asked me
It must feel good to be a single parent
Achieving at already having two high school graduates
I replied It's a feeling I can't explain
The world's longest ruler couldn't measure it
When I look at all my children
And see their many accomplishments
It's an emotion that brews up within
For as long as I live
The peak of my love will never descend
Someone asked me
Was there ever a moment that I've regretted
Do you ever wish you would have waited
I replied I wouldn't change a thing
Late teen when I had my first child
The other two followed shortly
The bible says "be fruitful and multiply"
So why regret what God gave me
He chose the perfect three
To be loved and cared for by me
I might have felt somewhat alone
But I was never by myself
For I gave them back to God long time ago
Knowing they'd be in perfect hands
This parenting road is mighty long

No detours, no dead ends
Laid a foundation very strong
At this rest stop that we call home
Wood and nails was my pain
Cement was my strength
I sweated joy and peace
Securing the perimeter with bricks
Built a chimney out of stone
To help ventilate any stress
Used slate on the roof
For longevity, making sure it last
Wood doors for the front and the back
Although expensive, I needed them
Because they're not easy to crack
Even though they had part- time fathers
Every day I clocked in
I remained a full- time mother
Didn't want to lose the benefits
Of watching the seeds I've loved and nourished
Become a successful young lady and two gentlemen

Mother

If it wasn't for you I wouldn't be here
So many times I forgot to mention
How much I love you my dear
There's nothing more in life
Than having a great mother
And I thank the Lord above
For you and my father to you I can express
The way that I feel
Because you have been my closest friend
Throughout all my years
You could always tell
If something isn't right
You could feel my pain
All through the night
When it's time to cry
You're the shoulder I lean on
You always comfort me
When life steers me wrong
You stayed up late nights
When I was on my last leg
Anything we wanted in life
We didn't have to beg
You are always there
Even when I decided to run wild
You prayed and you prayed
Never turning your back on your child

God Continue to Hover Over Me

It's hard to say goodbye to yesterday
I've been struggling and resisting
Trying to keep up with my Faith
For pain has returned with great luggage
I guess it's here to stay
God you said…"If we have the Faith the size of a
"mustard seed that we can move mountains"
I'm in the midst of my storms
It's feeling like you have abandoned me
Where you at, you supposed to be right here beside me
I'm at the very bottom So it don't matter
Might as well end all misery
Wrote two letters
One to the man I love, the other to my mommy
Explaining why I fail at love and how I love
Them, my children, siblings, and grand baby
Dropped them off and hit the highway
With no particular destination
Just looking for the right spot
To pull over and complete my final mission
I understand that I'm not perfect
I'm still out here sinning
Guess this the price I have to pay
For being very disobedient
You took everything away

Yes, this pain definitely got my attention
But this time I'm not strong
No means of carrying on
I need you Lord right now
Can't stand feeling all alone
So I called up my aunt Lilly
Needed someone powerful to pray with me
Lift me up out of this grey area
Thinking suicide and Lord knows
I know better
She said...
"That with the trying of our Faith brings forth great patience
And no matter which way I measure it
His Grace is very sufficient
The devil comes to steal, kill, and destroy
Since he didn't give it, don't let him steal your joy"
After all that crying
I felt in control again
God started revealing
All my Blessings that I had coming
So I'll just sit here and be patient
And receive everything that he has promised

Your Spirits Will Do

My heart has eyes
So I can still see you
For deep in my heart you lye
Your spirit is still here
It will never die
I feel your presence
Yet I do not fear
I give thanks to God that you are still here
Grandma Genola and Grandma Ola
You know I love and miss you two
You are always on my mind
I can never forget you
For you started our bloodlines
Both sides of my families
Are grounded in God, close- knit, and loving
We owe it all to you
For there would be none of us if it wasn't for you two
Grandpa Willie
Never have no doubt
Didn't come around much
But I forget you not
Uncle Sammie Lee
How are you
Don't believe we've formally met
But was told when I was a baby
On your chest my head rest

Said you rocked me to sleep, sung me lullabies
My son Sammie Lee is named after you
He even has your eyes My dear aunt Doris
You're the glistening to my sparkle
I remember all the things we use to do
Picnics, Wet & Wild, and Bush Gardens
Late nights swimming in your pool
You're the glistening to my sparkle
I remember all the things we use to do
Picnics, Wet & Wild, and Bush Gardens
Late nights swimming in your pool
Your smile was sent from Heaven
Your body is absent But Lord knows your spirit will do
Aunt Cookie My twin baby
They say I look like my daddy and you
And although we didn't spend much time together
In spirit you kept me close I want to thank you auntie
For all the talks we shared
I want to thank you for taking the time out, showing me you cared
Auntie Lil Ma Indeed we miss you
Still remember the grabbing of the arm
Whenever we acted a fool
I'll never forget the cleaning of the fish we would catch
And your house on the water front
Never beat around the bush
Kept it short, sweet, and blunt
In everything I do I keep ya'll in my mist
Although your bodies are absent
I thank the Lord for memories that we got to share

ARNIKIA ROBINSON

* The Down Fall OF Love Starts Here *

As If It Was Yesterday

It was exactly a year ago on this very same day
That my fiancé...asked for my hand in marriage
And it has not been one second out of these twelve months
That my answer to him has ever been regretted
It's all so fresh as if it was yesterday
Let me share with you the events that took my breath away
The phone rings, I answer
He says "babe what it do?" I say "Work"
He says "what are you doing after?"
I say "nothing much what's on your mind?"
He replies "Go home, freshen up,
and pick you up about nine"
I anxiously wait for 5 O'clock to come
Because hanging with my babe is always so much fun
Stepped in the house and when I was just about
To take my clothes off The doorbell rings
It's my neighbor with a single red rose
And a card that reads Head to the kitchen there's
something in the fridge for you So I do exactly what the card say
do There on the middle rack
Another red rose and a box of chocolates too
I go take a shower and get dressed as I planned
And at 8:48 pm my door bell rings again
There he stands with four more red roses in hand

The sun was setting as we begin to cruise
And when we pulled up to the lake
The shadow across the water was extremely beautiful
We walked up a dirt trail
To a spot he had prepared
Picnic baskets, scented candles, wine glasses, and a soft windy breeze
I turned around and found
Him down on one knee
Ring in hand and uttering
"Will you marry me?"
Quickly filled with emotions, I could not speak
Just nodded yes, covered my mouth, and let out a big scream
And when the car rolled up and my dad stepped out
Overflowing tears begin to stream down
And as daddy approached
I couldn't help but notice
Another dozen and a half of those single red roses
How did he get my dad and neighbor involved without me knowing
But at the end of the night
I ended up with two dozen of those good smelling roses
And so overwhelmed by the romance of my future husband
I mean it's all so fresh as if it was yesterday
Don't think the events of that night will ever fade away

Loyalty To My 3 Piece

You don't have to tell me how much it hurts

I already feel your pain

As a family we've been through so much

Nothing else to loose, everything to gain

I'll always be here till the end of this earth,

And Rewind it all back just to start all over again

Unfortunately we can't skip the bad sides

But there's also no rules that says we can't

Fast forward to the good times

Every now and then we'll

Pause to rest and gather ourselves,

because Once we hit play again

We'll continue to ride it out together

Till there's no wheels left

Found

Up high, down low
Or all around me
You're the glove
That fits me perfectly
I gave up on love
Because it was untrue to me
Guess I had to go through some things
In order to come to some things
Which was you
Never would I have dreamed
That you'd love me the way you do
I don't regret my past But the one I had last
Had me thinking that even love was unlovable
Then you came along
With your jazzy love song
Had me listening with no distractions
You have my full attention
When you're around
My heart starts missing...(you)
To the point that I close my eyes
To get a mental vision...(of you)
Trying to grasp the whole reason
Of why your so into me
But loving this space you got me in
First time visitor I've never been

Nowhere near this, it's refreshing
Can you promise to remain my everything
Always be honest because I can't afford to be hurt again
Let my guards down
Because you're nothing like war
You're my peace
From the battles that I've had before
You're my warmth
For other's left me out in the cold
You're my found
I'm not lost in love no more

A Woman's Worth

All I want is for a man To understand
The worth of a woman
After all she's responsible
For keeping our generations going
She's usually the glue
That keeps a family bond together
More precise description...
The woman was the one made from Adam's rib
For regeneration, as a companion, and
Most of all to represent unity and love
Woman should not be subjected
To mental, verbal, or physical abuse
Nor should she be rejected
Of equal opportunity when it comes to her loving you
Don't redirect her To a path that's uncertain,
dangerous, and irrelevant Keep your woman sheltered
With your warm and embracing arms
Every now and then tell her
How you love having her around It won't hurt
anything to share it how she completely benefits
You For a woman Is the closest thing to Heaven
On this earth that you'd come to
And no, a woman worth can't be measured
There's no scale built to tell us
Why being a woman is so valuable

Christel O. Valentine
Don't think I ever
Got the chance to tell ya
Good bye...
As a matter of fact I know I didn't
You didn't want me to know and I don't know why
You was like another one of my sister's
Through any and everything I was by your side
Close to you like I am my religion
So when you got sick
Why wasn't my number dialed
I'm still pondering over that question
Once told me that
You love me, your god son, and family
But you didn't want us to worry
I told you that
When two people share a bond quite like we do
Your story became my story
Whatever it was that you were going through
Why not call on me
I would have went through it too
That's something we knew about one another
All those times I had to call on you
So many times you had to be in my corner
Thinking back to our last Christmas
I remember brushing your hair; you were too tired and restless
I tried to quickly flee

You opened your eyes saying
"Oh you are leaving me?"
I said
"I was dipping out because you are falling asleep"
You formed and grin and said
"No I wasn't"
I laughed and said
"Christel cut it out you were snoring"
Friend I even remember our last conversation And I'm thinking to
myself that I would have called everyday
Up until that very last day
When I received the phone call at 5 O'clock in the morning
Knew something was wrong right away
KB never rung my line that early
So my first reply was
"Good morning and what's wrong with your mother?"
Then I let out such an enormous cry
Surprise it didn't wake my neighbors
The news she delivered changed my life
From that moment all the way until forever
Who's gone be my best friend now
Who's gone give me straight advice
Who'll know what to do when I'm down

To lift my spirits back high What friend will I trust in
As a reference on the school's emergency contact list
What friend will love my babies as if they were hers
Who's going to always answer her phone
No matter what time I call
I came into the knowledge now
That everything has a season
You were here to show me how
True friends love unconditionally
I'll forever hold on to our bond, and the many of life lessons
But most of all...
I'll forever hold on to your love and darling friendship

Let's Have A Threesome (With This Love Song)

DJ want you play this girl a love song
So sick and tired of twerking
I want to slow it down
Body rock for a second
Turn this fast pace intimate
Rest my head in his chest
Begin to seize the moment
Interlock my hands with his
Literally no space in between us
The music to my ears
Should sound a little like this
I want the beat to thump
So bold and beautiful
I want the chord to be strong
Since it consist of three notes
And the durational patterns
To even out with comparison
I need the melodies to sound out
So meticulous and meaningful
The lyrics should come across
So lustful and loveable
I want the rhythm to sound off

So remarkable and recurring
So our performance arts scale
Can keep frequently moving
Up to the tempo of love
This keeps our pitch sounding smoothly
When hitting articulations
Oooh (second wind)
DJ repeat that love song for us

That Type of Loving

I want to be his sun as well as his moon
Want his love to cover me as deep and as wide
As the universe
He'll lift my spirit and soul so high
That it'll feel like I've touched Heaven
And when we stare in each other's eyes
I want to see nothing but sparkling stars
As me
In his pupil's reflection
I want him to hold me tight, that
It feels like he squeezed the entire Solar System together
I want that planet rock, outer space, and beyond kind of love
I want my mind to get Alzheimer's
At the mentioning of an ex
For he erased all bad memories and changed me for the best
To where I only want to remember him as if
He has always been my first and only
He'll make my heart jump a beat
And skip to his tune when he's next to me
Send chills up my spine
Every time I see him smile or grin
I exhale a deep breath of contentment
Because security from him is what I breath back in
My stomach can't digest this feeling that I'm feeling
It's tangled up, tied up, tossing, and turning

My knees get weak to where my feet
Is no longer good for standing
All of my body systems are confused
They can't comprehend what is happening
My inner body and soul is saying "Don't stop"
And it won't stop until it has reached the outer surface
On my skin I see goose bumps
Yeahhh....
I want that mind, body, and soul type of loven.

Comparison

If I had to name his love after a country
I would call it Africa
And if I had to be more specific
Let's say Kenya, Africa
For it lies along the Indian Ocean
Which minds me of how our love
Keeps flowing and flowing
Just like the ripples in its water
Because they're endless and ongoing
Sits slightly above the equator
Which splits our globe in half
Reminding me of the 50/50 rule that me and him share
There's no mine, there's no yours
Only the words
Together or Ours
With Ethiopia to the North, Somalia to the Northeast
Uganda to the West, and Tanzania to the South
They make up a strong, thick border
That protects it all around
That's just like the core of our relationship
So sturdy that no one can tear, rip or break it
Going inland of Kenya you see amazing Savannah grasslands
And just like that landscape

No one's more tall, cute, and handsome than my man
Named after Mount Kenya, a significant landmark
And second among Africa's highest mountain peak
Just like the peak that I reach
When he makes love to me
Like the water that starts to boil while heating on the stove
My emotions and juices begin to overflow
He's touching my body
And it's something like a metaphor
I feel his hands sinking pass my skin
And now they're touching my soul
Forever holding me tight and never letting me go
They say there, the sun shines all year round
I say, here, I can relate
For there's no cloudy days in our way
Just like the consistency of its tropical and arid climate
Our love, too, stays the same
Kenya is the setting for migration of the great wildebeest
Reminds me of the sexual beast that erupts out of me
That's only a side that he gets to see
For I'm a lady in the streets, freak in the sheets
So loving my man is like getting some African history
About one of its most populate, beautiful, and largest
cities...Kenya

O' Happy Days

Someone once told me
That you being happy isn't fair
I hate that you enjoy the bright side of life
While I sit in darkness
Have you ever been there
I see you always smiling and boasting
While I pretend just to fit in
I smile on the outside
Blink constantly to hide my hollow eyes
My heart cry on the inside
I've become a pro at covering up my lies
Can you imagine feeling this way
Walking around like every day is a good day
(When it's not)
Once again you being happy isn't fair
Do you have enough of that joy
That you can share
Ask me on any given day, I'll never be caught off guard
I'll know exactly what to say
For I study my lines
Concentrate hard on my behavior
So you'll never see my true feelings or figure me out
Did God play Tic-Tac-Toe amongst us

He "O" so loved the good ones
And "X" out all the rest of us
Would we be considered the bad ones
So many grey days
Think the sun is scared to shine on us
You being happy oh so isn't fair
But I'm willing to give up everything
Leaving, all that I have and own
To be right beside you, happy over there

Helper

My mouth promised to never help them again
So why is my mouth and heart conflicting
Plenty of times I spoke it
But every time my heart broke it
Leaving me with a severe case of broken promises
I'm listening Lord
What are you trying to tell me
Got my eyes wide open
Catching a glimpse of everything you want me to see
Hopefully...
Why does everyone's pain actively affect me
I just can't do it, can't stand not to help
When there's someone out there who needs me

Love

Love is like
A flower that blossoms in the sun
Love is like
Laughter when people are having fun
Love is like
A walk on the beach
When two people are being romantic
Love is like
Pregnancy when husband and wife has planned it
Love is like
The pretty skies that sit so high above
Love is like
A piece of god that never gets dull
Love can also be the opposite
When people treat you like dirt
Some people just don't care
How easy one's feelings can hurt
Love can make you look stupid
Giving all that you can give
Love can make you commit suicide
Thinking there's no reason to live
Love could be good or bad
Make you blind so you can't see
I'm speaking from experience
Because once love took over me

Finding Myself

It's been a long time coming
But I'm finally feeling like the woman
That I was meant to be
I mostly over it all to you
For you're the change that changed me
Folk say I'm glowing
Because they not knowing
What has got into me
For they see a new person
Not the little shy Nicky
That covers her face when she is smiling
Or the one who wore baggy clothes
Rejecting the fact that her shape was appealing
The one who wore silky weave
Her natural roots was too nappy
She hated her government name
Said it sounded too African
Wanted to bleach the color of her skin
Thought she had to be lighter to fit in
Her eyes are not hazel
They're actually dark brown
Her face was too fat and round
She carried that hate
For whom she was around for awhile
Then one day I crossed paths with you
The person who let me know that

Who I am inside and out is beautiful
To never ever doubt myself again
Because if I can take your eyes
And see myself through them
That I'll be looking at pure perfection
For God made
Each and every one of us different
And we're all his children and special creations
I fell in love with myself that day
Right along with falling in love with you
Thank you for helping me appreciate me

I learned

As you grow older
You see things differently
Your thoughts become more mature
Not only in age but you grow in wisdom
And your knowledge becomes broader
I learned
That when I see BS coming
I stop it in its tracks
And I can actually keep quiet
For my silence is my greatest attack
I learned
There are three sides to every story
Between the two and then the truth
Only God knows the final verdict
So who am I to be judging you
I learned
Some people are just nosey
Everyone don't really care about you
Or what you're going through
They just want to evaluate your story
I learned
My very best will have to do
Can't offer what I don't have
Decreasing the stress that has me bound
Increasing how to love, live, and laugh
I learned

Even if I help a multitude
Some would still say I haven't done enough
And if I want to configure the weight of my blessings
I'll just measure it by the strength of my burdens
I learned
It's okay to not know everything
Because every learning experience is a great thing
Life lessons teaches us daily
So I'll continue to wear my whole armor fully
I'M GLAD I'M STILL LEARNING

My Love For You

Like opened floodgates of Heaven
Rain down blessings
Overflowing...is my love for you
Visions of the sun rising
In the morning
My love...I think of you
Walking on the beach
While in the sand my feet sink
So deep...is my love for you
Hot oils, gentle hands Full body massaging
Caressing...is my love for you
In the park after dark
Slow pace jogging
Exercising...my love for you
Inhale, hold it, and now exhale
Deep breathing Relaxing...is my love for you
Aqua waters from Jamaica
So soothing Everlasting...is my love for you
Side by side, arms wrapped around
Slightly squeezing Cuddling...is my love for you
Keep me here, freeze this moment
Don't want to lose it
Longevity...is what I'm praying for in you

Loving You Is Like

Loving you is like
Waking up every morning with the sun shining in your face
At that moment thanking God once again for his Grace
Loving you is like
When you see a butterfly land on your shoulder
You appreciate a life so free and beautiful
Loving you is like
Jumping up on the morning of Christmas
Cupid made no mistake when he aimed his bow and arrow at us
Loving you is like
Joy and pain of experiencing childbirth
Every moment I see your face, outweighs all hurtful moments
Loving you is like
Looking through clear Bahamas waters
How perfectly clear is the future that lies before us
Loving you is like
Lyrics of your most favorite love song
Keeping it on repeat because the words hit so close to home
Loving you is like
Going to a lot and purchasing a new car
Tender loving care is what will carry us very far
Loving you is like
Buying a brand new house
Always letting me into your world, never locking me out

Long Time Coming

It's been a long time coming
That I finally got our unity
To where it needs to be
I've waited a long time
To feel like his pride and joy
I feel like I've just ran and smashed
The 400 yard dash
At his track meet
He finally decided to crown me
With the gold medal and the first place trophy
It's been a long time coming
Officially I'm his one and only woman
Parading me in public
No longer hiding me from friends and family
I love it
Tell me who wouldn't
It's a great feeling on the inside
To complete a task that I found so challenging
At last,
Don't have to compete with any other female species
It's finally all about me
But I stayed with patience
Other's thought I should have given up a long time ago
But to me he was worth waiting for
Because good things come to those who wait, and
It's been a long time coming

Suitable

If I ask you to hold me
Would that be too much
Hold me and never let me go
For I love to meditate on the softness of your touch
Ever so gentle
Never so rough
My brain gets romanced, when I get to thinking
About your perfect being
No flaws at all
Got me studying
Your every move because
There's got to be something
About you that can piss me off
I know I should not be expecting it (the bad)
Because when you got something this good
You should accept it
But this feeling is sort of scary
For in past relationships
I've been
Beat down, stomped on, and neglected
To where being loved by a real man
Seems so anorexic
But anorexic in a good way
To where I lose all appetite when he's in sight
Try kicking it with my friends
Only to find myself thinking about him

If he was in the ocean filled with sharks
I'd still be willing to take that swim
For I feel safe in his arms
More secure in this relationship
Than any I've ever been
I'm thirsty for his loving
So let me give you a brief description
If I was a coffee lover
He'd be my sugar and French Vanilla flavor
If I loved tea, then he'd be green tea
Because all of his organics is what's good for me
If I was an alcoholic referrer
He'll be like no other
Than the gin that makes you sin
For my water twisters
He's that ice cold chiller
That I'd be sipping to quench my thirst from within

Respect Yourself

It's morning laying here next to him
But have nothing to show for it
Except for some
Open condom wrappers and my gapped legs
I would blame it on the alcohol
But the liquor is no excuse
For the way I'm acting
Walking around talking about
They better respect this
How am I going to get respect
If I drop my panties
For every Tom, Dick, and Harry
It feels good for the moment
After I'll flaunt it
We end up in the bedroom
With him climbing up on me
Taking care of my body
Fulfilling my needs
My eyes rolling, got me moaning
Now he's finished
Slowly climbing off of me
My mind and body becomes enemies
That's when my conscious kicks in
Making me feel dirty and like a fool

For allowing this to keep happening
Over and over again
The thought is sickening
Because I don't consider myself a hooker or prostitute
So what category do I fit in
Should I be given a special label too
Sex supposed to be special
You can't just give it away
Because at the end of the day
You should be able to look in the mirror and say
I love and respect that face

Not No One Night Stand

You can't leave until I tell you to leave
Think you can come in here
Touch me, kiss me, and make love to me
Then like a convict on the run
Pack your bags and leave
No baby these sheets right here come with lock and key
See once you opened up the surprise
Of this cherry pie between my thighs
I locked you down for the rest of the night
Shoot, maybe the next 3, 4, or 5
I don't recall the plan
Where we discussed a one night stand
My motto is simple
Make love to me, and then make love to me some more
Then I'll decide rather if and when you can go
Nooo…
I'm not trying to make you love me
But you will respect me as a lady
Not treating me like no hoe
Especially if you did not pay me
Don't want your cash
Just a good ole smash
So all those toot it and boot it
Wham bam, thank you ma'am
Gets no play

Need to please me to my liking
Then I'll send you on your way
But there's a saying that sounds a little classier
I don't care what no one says
Liking the sound of "Friends with benefits"
The difference is
You get some time, loving, and special gifts

"X" Out The "O"

Do me a favor
Don't do me any favors
Dealing with you is like playing
Tic-Tac-Toe
Trying to see who'll play last
And land the winning score
Not putting anyone else priorities
Before mine anymore
I made a straight line
That's three in a row
So the winner got to be me
Because no longer am I willing
To deal with your multiple personalities
You're an immature and ungrateful somebody
Who needs to develop
A grown-ups mentality
For some of your ways
Are still elementary and childish
And the one's that applaud you
Only do so
Because y'all share some common similarities
In other words

You need to pick your peers more wisely
Let's get clarity
Reaching out to me
Is like doing me a favor
So go on with your life
You're always so dramatically
Total opposites, nothing alike
Your plate stays full
Of problems, misery, and strife
That's why I'm X'ing out all the O's

I'm Tired

I'm tired
Of all this fighting
I'm tired
Of all this mess
I'm tired
Of going crazy
But I'm not tired of being blessed
I'm tired
Of feeling guilty
I'm tired
Of all this lying
I'm tired
Of feeling down
I'm tired
Of all this crying
I'm tired
Of this whole relationship
I'm tired
Of feeling blue I'm tired

Of all this arguing and not knowing what to do
I'm tired
Of feeling stupid
I'm tired
Of feeling dumb
I'm tired
Of trying to explain to you just where I'm coming from
I'm tired
Of you specifically
I'm tired
Of your heart not being real
I'm tired
Of you not caring exactly how I feel
I'm sick and tired of being tired

Colliding Worlds

Laying on my back
Head looking toward the sky
Wishing upon every star
That I see passing by
Want to snap my fingers and
Meet them in that blue yonder franchise
An out of body experience right now
Would suit me just fine
Tired of getting knocked down
Each and every time I try
I have no clue on what you want me to do
I take a step forward
You push me back two
I'm trying to imagine
What in the hell is happening
One breath you want me involved
Next breath you're not having it
Now you're looking discombobulated

Because I done silenced, not answering
Feels like I showed up to a party
Without a personal invitation
Don't like including me in your world
But I always include you in mine
Like vinegar and oil
We not mixing, can't combine
So what I'll do
Is sit back and play it cool
My thoughts and feelings are a wreck
So if I shut down, don't get upset

Taking A Stand

It confusing…relationships
Is it worth giving…your all
If you're not taking…nothing away from it
I'll start rebuking
And like Martin Luther King
I have a dream
To always stay true to me
So that's when I'll start refusing
To get caught up in his web of lies and deceit
I'm like Kunta Kinte, when he says
"My name not Toby"
And continue to get beat
Because just like him
I'll always stand firm on what I believe
I'm not submitting…when the master speaks
Something like Rosa Parks
Not only black power but woman power
I be durn if a man makes me feel less then he
I'll walk beside you but not behind you
Gone always speak my mind
Not only when given permission to
The bible says
"Do unto others as you would have them do unto you"

That's not only for neighbors
But relationships too
See some men are trips
When they get on their ego-trips
Thinking it's a man's world and
No woman has a place in it
Wait...Yes she do
But only for her to serve and cater to him
That's when women should turn Harriet Tubman
Jumping on the first Underground Railroad...escaping
Leaving his durn self to deal with him

Can I Talk To You

Can you give me one second
So I can talk to you
For there's something I want to say
But you making it hard to do
For when you see me, you turn the other way
I know actions speak louder than words
And with my actions I've let you down
You don't know how much I'm missing you
Now that you're not around
You think I'm living while you're hurting
Vice Versa
I'm hurting while you're living
I see that you have moved on
For that I can't be mad
I know you're treating her just like you treated me
Like an African Beauty Queen
And I'm missing that so bad
In life you're taught many of lessons
I'll take this as a lesson learned
I labeled you "Good man of the century"
Because that title you have earned
I know some days you think of me
You know she's not what you want
So when that day comes that you are free
I'll be waiting for you to come and rescue me

Shut In

You should keep your feelings
All bundled inside
Be strong you can take it
Just go for the ride
It's easier said than done
When you haven't walked the mile
Because it's easier to frown
Than to give a big smile
You live your life and then you die
You go through trials and tribulations
But you don't know why
You're shut in, you've shut out
That's the way that it goes
It's so easy to withdraw
When you can't take no more
Everything is not peaches and cream
On the outside looking in
At the time of lending a hand
Just where are your friends
You're shut in, you've shut out
But there's one subject I haven't discussed
What are the odds, because there are no evens
Of you and your mate to constantly fuss
It's not worth the burden that you carry within
Because you're only hurting your health
When you become shut in

Agree

It's been heavy on my mind
And I need to stop by
So we can discuss our relationship
No phone convo, need eye contact
While we attack
Some of the things we having problems with
This can only go on for so long
Without us reaching an agreement
Everything you say or do
Will not sit right with me
And everything I say or do
Won't make you happy
But that's the beauty of us two
Getting to learn one another
Weathering the ups and the downs
So we end up on the same level
I'm more than willing to take this ride
If you'd be my seat belt
Strap me in, hold me down tight
For those bumpy roads ahead
And if you get tired
Can't stand on your own then I'd be your backbone
Promise to never leave your side

You'd never stand alone
Some days we'll agree to disagree
Just don't give up on me
Since nothing in this life is free
Look at the bond that we share as an investment
The more we put in
The more we'll get out of this accomplishment
Even if the sky come tumbling down
We'll make the best of it
Show the world that we strike hard
Just like a closed fist

Appreciating Myself

I know in your eyes
I'm not the baddest chick walking this earth
But I'm more than content with my
Beautiful face, plus size waist, and spicy curves
It's not solely about being pretty
Or my outside physique I'm excited about the
beauty on the inside of me because the rarest form
is only skin deep At times it seems
As if you're trying to lower my self esteem
With the little things that you be saying Like… "There's always a
girl out there that looks better than yours" 'or'
"You making me think that your God's gift to the world"
Don't think I'm special but I am a gift
And I get it
Something's I shouldn't tell, should keep it to myself
Just a part of me always feels the need to share
And there's somebody out there looking
Better than me to you
Then there's those that think I'm out here looking
Better to them then they girl too
But let me point out that whenever you're down
I try to build you back up
Rather it's with your finances
Even when you don't approve of your looks
Just know I'm not conceited
Because you don't know how long it took
For me to even accept or appreciate my good looks

I Am Who I Am

To you I may not be the best
My hair may not fall down past my neck
My eyes may be simple, not colorful
And my nose may be square
But I am who I am
Because that's how my God made me
I may be a shade darker in my skin
May be a little plump, nothing close to slim
My fingers may look like tree stumps
No nails, because I've bitten them all off
Have no full cheek bones
And my chin may be a little long
But I am who I am
Because that's how my God made me
I may not have a song to sing
No favorite verse in any poem that I read
You may not see model material when you look at me
May not be a leader, just not fit to lead
But I am who I am
Because that's how my God made me
My teeth may not be pearly white
Have a smile that may not shine bright
Fall short a few inches in my height

You may say I look wrong
But I know I'm just right
Because I am who I am
And that's how my God made me
SO who am I to question my creator
Never will I walk around ungrateful
He may have given you some features
That he did not give to me
Either take me as I am or let me be
Because I am who I am
Exactly how my God made me

It's About

Have you ever felt like
Maybe you're not the one for him
Often times when you're in public
Another beautiful woman
Walks by and he begins to stare
Not flat out looking
Of course he tries to do it on the low
As if you're stupid
Of course he hoping it doesn't show
I've been noticed
In case you didn't know
And no one's perfect
But I already predicted the next line you'll say to me
"Baby I'm only human"
No problem you can look
Just don't look while you're walking with me
To who requires much respect
Much respect should be given
How would you like it
If I stared and went into a daze
Behind that strong, black, fine brother
That keeps passing my way
If someone can catch your attention like that
To where it disrespects
The woman you're with

Then that's where you need to be at
It's not about being insecure
It's about behaving proper
It's not about having low self esteem
It's about protecting your mate's feelings
Because when it comes to me
When I'm in public with you
No other man can grasp my attention
BUT YOU'RE ONLY HUMAN RIGHT? WELL SO AM I!!

Baby Momma Drama

I wouldn't give a half a cent
For what you're stressing
I know you're his baby momma
For I, myself fits in that category
But I, myself don't cause any drama
Just because I'm with your child's father
Don't mean I'm giving you the highest honor
Of respect
For you have to give in order to receive that back
And quit putting your child in the middle of our beef
They have nothing to do with that
You want them to dislike me
Because you be on that childish shit
The math problem is real simple
But I'll still break it down for you
Adding your baby daddy to my life
Gave me nothing but love for them
But you can subtract the bickering and strife
That there I'm not about to deal with
Not wanting to replace you as they mother
I have my own set of kids
I actually don't get this

Why do parents try to make the step parents
So miserable
You can't name one thing that I've personally done towards you
Except that now I'm with this man that you once had
So you gone share with me all of his negative mishaps
Because his good definitely don't outweigh his bad
And if that's the case
You should be glad I took him off your hands
Instead you frown your face
And try and make certain demands
Thinking that because you're his baby momma
Your title carries weight
Well not over here ma'am
One thing for certain
Is that I'm a grown woman
So I'm going to make sure he cares for his seeds
All this extra that you coming with
Needs to be piped down and deceased
Grow up, act your age, and remember your place
Because that title that you so happily carry
Is pretty much every woman's case
Almost everybody has a baby daddy
And by yours, you've been replaced
I'm not your child's enemy
You'd know if you get to know me
Gone treat them as if they were mine
And I love mines unconditionally

Frustrated

The most frustrating part of this
Is when you know what you know
The respect for your feelings
They care less to show
Wondering should I go ahead and tell him how I know
More than what he thinks I know
Or should I just leave it alone
For he knows it isn't right
But instead of saying "I'm sorry"
He continues to put up a fight
Guess he can never be wrong in his eyes
Put one of those shoes on my foot
I would be treated like a crook
That robbed someone's heart
It'll be a never ending story
Until I openly
Confessed to my part
Me, on the other hand will take it all in
Because the longer I wait
The better the expression would be on his face
When he realize that I have evidence
No he say/she say
See they have a lot to say
If and when the disloyalty is on the other person

But when it falls back on them
They refuse to answer any of your questions
Why not?
We just had a two hour conversation
About what I supposedly done wrong
Looks like that things that I was accused of
You've been doing all along
So how does the kettle call the pot black
Where do you see justice in all of that
How can you be 100% with me
When you're not 100% with yourself
I found cracks in your foundation
Can't build a honest relationship there
Cracks of lies
Sour riddles and fake lullabies
Cracks of cheating
Trying to hook up with other women
While claiming to be in love with me
Cracks of deceit
Frequently misleading
Cracks of stubbornness
For when you're wrong
You're not even man enough to admit to it

Nothing Personal

I gave it everything I had
So why should I feel bad
About letting go
I had great plans for us
Didn't love anyone else
But you
In my picture frame (my mental frame)
Were pictures of a good life
But in my private closet (during my lonely hours)
Were conversations of me pleading with God
To bring us closer together
Thought that any storm we can weather
As long as in the end it turned us out for the better
We were like diamonds in the rough
And in order to get us
Where we needed to be
I withstood the pressure
PRESSURE... (I like that)
Because no matter how rough it got
I stood ten toes flat
May have swayed a bit
Encountered a few turns and bends
But never did I completely fold
I don't know what you've been told
Because good women don't come a dime a dozen

There's very few of us
And I'm one of them
The one that you messed over
No one took your woman
You practically gave me away
Think about what you say
Love…
Well your love slapped me in the face
Look up the meaning of that word
Before you fix your mouth to utter that word
For when you actually get a full understanding of it
Then you'll know that was something that you wasn't capable of
Even if you did love me
What the hell of a way to show me
What messed it all up
Was the moment I realized
What I was worthy of

I'm All To The Good

Round of applause
For such a hell of a performance
Because now you want it
Back when I tried to give you my affection
You act like I wasn't worth it
The love and respect I had for you
Was damn sho flaunted
Let no other feast on this panty pie
Had your name all upon it
Stayed faithful to you
And I don't know why
Because you didn't deserve it
Had to make reservations
Just to get time with you
Looking back, man was I tripping
How do you think that made me feel
Oh, I'm eager to tell
Like when a credit card that gets declined
When you trying to pay a bill
So embarrassing on couple's night
When the only one missing was you
So there I were the 5th leg
You cut your phone off
Oops correction….
Your battery went dead

Unreachable...
You're very disrespectful
On the outside looking in
No one knows what I've been through
For I held my head high, on my lips formed a grin
That's the word defined as pretend
Nowhere near a perfect mate
Don't even consider you a close friend
That thin line between love and hate
Something you can't mend
So let me interrupt your session
With me taking a bow
I'm all to the good
No need in missing me now

Going Down

Broken down with shattered hopes
Figuring out why love feels so useless
Delusions and anxiety in overload
Even fantasy land is reach less
Medicated to the highest point
Because depression is nothing to play with
Transformations of my body trying to cope
With this bruised heart that he has left me with
Calgon take me to another place, but
No dreamland because I'm restless
Throw heartache in a river
Watch if float away
Praying someone crack the bottle
And read the message
But even then, I'm wondering can I be saved
Or am I too far gone beyond repairing
Prep, transfuse, and revive me
With units of love, self-worth, and security
Then transfer me to a rehab facility
So that I can start my quick recovery
Let the staff teach, so I can learn again
What true love feels like
And begin to live again

HIM

I would like to take the time out to say thank you
To HIM
The guy that was in my life
That I thought would be here for the rest of my life
Y'all know the type (that makes you think)
That all the other's went left
Because he's the only one right
He's heaven sent so HE should be idolized
No longer would a sister have to worry about
Abuse, cheating, and lies (right right)
So let me take a moment to applaud him
For playing with my mind
You know ladies, that "I KEEP IT REAL" mankind
But in this field I'm a "G"
I know pain to the third degree
Like I know my ABC's I'm a conquer mentally
Have taken punches and bruises physically
But yet I still stand
Hurt will never defeat me
Can't focus on the negativity
Or I would think that there's no more love out there to be lost
Or shall I say found
For one day the right one will come around
So I would like to take the time out to say thank you
To HIM

Some things are better left unsaid
Some lies I'd rather not hear
If you wanted to layup, for a couple of months
And not give me a for sure thing
You knew I was just an "in the moment" thing
Then you should have just said that
Skin like alligator baby, I could have dealt with that
I know pain to the third degree
You're not the first one to ever mistreat me, but
Eventually
Your time will come
Karma is a female dog
Always looking to have a little fun
On your playground is where she'll play and stomp
Then you tell me how you'll feel
For when she comes knocking at your door
You'll know that shit just got real
When you get to calling her phone and she don't answer
You won't even know how to deal
Or when every dude number in her phone
Is her cousin
Yet and still
That lie so old it was invented before the windmill
(Y'all HIM is something else for real)
So let me take the time out to say thank you
To MR. HIM

I Want To Know

I once read a story entitle SHMILY
See How Much I Love You
And every time I think of that story
It reminds me of you
For I realized that fairy tales may not always come true
Which is cool Because my love is actual
No riddles or rhymes
Don't begin with once upon a time
Instead it begins with...
I want to know
Because I want to know
Are you willing to slow dance with me
Can we start this relationship out slow
Are you willing to build trust with me
Some more things that I need to know
That when you lead me on this dance floor
Would it be safe to close my eyes and just glide
I trust you not to let me fall
For it's a must that every relationship have security
They'll be some things that we may not understand
But like Mr. Miyagi showed Danielson
It was a lesson in Wax On and Wax Off

Of course it didn't make sense then
But in the end
We'll be some polished champions
Not expecting everything to be grand
Just assure me that in our hard times
You'll never let go of my hands
Promise to love me in places I've never been
Loved before And unlike Siamese twins
Don't care to be joined at your hip
As long as our hearts are compatible
Are you God- fearing, family- oriented, and do you have patience
Can you be honest, caring, and forgiving
I need to know will you be willing to listen,
with your undivided attention Can you be loyal
Rate me on nothing less than my dedication, devotion, and
potential for this is a journey that
I've never traveled before I'm not looking for no
Million dollar man financially just do
the very best you can
Don't forget we are a couple
This means together we are a team
And if one of us gets weak or begin to lean
The other would be that strong post
See together we have to be all in
So let me say this once again for I want to know
For I want to know are you willing to slow
dance with me Start this relationship out slow
As my partner provide everything I need
While I'm slow grinding to your beat...on this dance floor

Hello

Hello
Can you hear me
Can you see me
I'm trapped in this maze
Trying to find my way to freedom
Been here for days
And every corner that I'm turning
Is leading to dead ends
Come rescue me
This life I don't like living
Hello
Help me out of here
No longer want to be here
Waking up every morning panting
From dreams so scary (nightmare land)
Sweating
So hard that I'm
Wetting
My bed sheets
This maze is confusing
I need help to solve this problem
Hello
Can you hear me
Can you see me
Guide me to the door that can free me

Every room has locked doors
I can't take this no more
Why me?
Give me the key to sanity
So I can unlock it
Somebody please stop it
The voices in my head
Mentally block them
The memories that got me afraid
To lift my head high in society
Please repair this broken frame
That made my pictured no longer perfect
Voices go away
I need help to correct it
Simplify this maze
And keep me uplifted
I'm sure I'll find my way
For God saves all his children

Revisiting The Past

Walking on cloud 9

Hurt and pain trying to pull me back down

To level ground

But love keeping me afloat

I promise to never see those days any more

Loving me is what matters most

Not traveling back down memory lane

The past is the past

I care less to visit that place again

Let me share my story (so you'll know what happened)

It was a very dark circle

I felt like on the movie "Bubble Boy"

When the little boy was trapped in the plastic bubble

The more I tried to leave

The harder I'd stumble

I feel him right there breathing down on me

I smell the steam coming from his nose

He's mad and upset and it very well shows

One mighty strong fist

That made my left eye close

A follow up hit to the corner of my lip

Busting it open, letting the blood flow

I did a quick flinch

When he put the 9 milli to my dome

Saying "Now let's play a little game called
Russian Roulette, and before I pull this trigger
I'm going to give you a chance to escape
You better hope this chamber is the wrong one
Because if it's not then all bets are done"
So I took out fast
Didn't feel my feet touching the grass
Yeah he put on a chase, but Couldn't catch me
Wasn't giving him the pleasure of killing me that day
I'm speaking out loud asking
"God what's wrong with this creature?"
Because he can't be a human
Only wild animals hunt you down like prey
That's why when I got away, I stayed away
Hmm...well I guess it's okay
To travel back down memory lane
To keep me reminded of a place
I never want to visit again

Whom Shall It Be

I know they hate they love me
At times I hate it to
Wish I could have been anyone else besides me
I'm tangled in this love triangle
Catching heat of 90 degrees at every angle
I'm so confused
Don't know what to do
I'm not torn between the two
I'm torn in between the three
Not that I love all of them
But that they all love me
I've been as truthful as I can be
Never misleading
Won't tell them what they want to hear
But what they need to know
Since I have to choose one
Then which two am I willing to let go
The decision is hard, because they all work hard
To get and keep my attention
Although this is not a contest
It's a three way decision
This game on dead lock
All of them are winning

This makes it very tough
But what if in my choosing
I end up loosing
They might be showing me just what I need to see
Then once they have me
The story scene will change
That's why I hate gambling in this game
You can hit the big bucks
Or end up
With pocket change

The Blues

Got a call one morning saying
I couldn't call you last night because the phone was off
And who have you been riding around with
Are you messing off on me,
Are you kicking it with your baby daddy?"
If me and you are in a relationship
There should be no other man in the passenger seat
I know we're living in different households
But we're still together
And for the last couple of days
You seem more distant now, then when I was there
Yes, someone told me I been seeing you girl riding
And we didn't know how to tell ya
But the man riding with her, wasn't you
So do you know how embarrassing
How much I felt like a fool I love you
And I moved out so I can better myself for you
But this is the thanks I get
This is how you do
Well I guess it's over between us two
I would like to remain friends
Because one day we'll cross each other paths again
For I can't lie, you are a good woman
But right now I'm done with relationships
For no one knows how to be faithful

Tender Kiss's vs. Manly Fist's

What did I do to deserve this
One moment he kissing me with his lips
Next he hitting me with his fist
Don't understand this type of love
For I've never been in a relationship like this
One day I want to run, one day I want to stay
He showers me with gifts
Thinking that'll take the pain away
Wish he'd use more of his tender kisses
And less of his manly fist's
When trying to get his point across
He builds me up
Just to tear me back down
Looking in the mirror at times
I feel like Bozo the clown
He spends 100 of dollars on MAC make up
So I can cover up
When family and friends come around
With a smile on my face and shoulder's spread wide
I hold my head high
When I step outside
No no no...

The world must never know
How much I've cried
But when I come back inside of this place I call home
Wash away the cover up
Just to see the lumps and bruises on my dome
I get all torn up
With his type of love
Should I run or should I stay
Will he use his tender kisses or manly fist's
To show how much he cares for me today

Something For Nothing

So you're the woman he been kicking it with
The real reason to why he has to work late
Or take company trips out of town every other weekend
As if I lack all common sense
After a while when things calmed down
I just played along with it
Because I knew eventually my man would slip
And that I proved, because one night when he got drunk
I talked him into giving me the password to his cell phone
Went straight to the text messages
And there was the communication
Between him and Andre, aka Ms. Andrea
Reading all 52 correspondeses
Thinking to myself
"Oh this keeps getting better and better"
From woman to woman
There are some things I'd like to know
Like how could you have felt even a little important
When a man would only enter through your back door
See he tried to go unnoticed
Couldn't dare risk his wife and kids at home
In which you knew about
Because in your 5th message, 3rd line from the top
You asked my husband
Was he ever getting a divorce or moving his stuff out

Just another thing that I would like to discuss
What made you think that a side dish like you
Could fill my man up
I'm the full course meal
The appetizer, main entrée, and the desert
Could care less about how you feel
Now that you realize he's never giving his family up
Because I also read it
In your little text confessions
When you said it
"I'm in love with you but your still in love with her"
See, in this man much I've invested
My marriage not about to crumble now
I won't give you that much credit
For falling in love with a married man
Your broken heart will be your punishment
And his will be guilt
For his conscience will never let him forget it

He Don't Need Me

I'm struggling to listen
To my heart that's beating
So silently
And the place where my veins and arteries meet
Should have a beat that thumps loudly
But yet it whispers
Like an echo at the end when it fades
Or a person speaking low asking
"What did he say?"
To the person next to them in church
On any given Sunday
What's wrong with this picture
I'm sitting here without a frame
Making one last wish, like a death row convict
Facing prosecution day
To get injected and within seconds
His life is taken away
Did I mention
That the dimensions of my soul are so hollow and deep
I keep filling this cylinder but cannot reach
The peak of my feelings
How could this be
I feel like hands are around my neck
Squeezing tightly, oh so tightly
Till every last breath slowly escape my body

Is it you or is it me
That's making me doubt if you really love me
I'm yelling, can you hear me
Getting hoarse from screaming repeatedly
Now I have no voice
Guess I'll mimic what it is that I'm saying
Or will you see it a little better
If I act it out in a one- act play
But I understand that you're just a man
Showing your love the best way you can
Hmm.....
Making me feel secure was never in the plan 'err
A woman should never feel that a man
Cares for, loves, or even needs her.

Message From The Wise

Men are the men that love me
Although they don't personally know me
They could only know of me
Because my name floats about as a great fix
A fix of pleasure for the ones
Who wants to fill sexual desires
Without having to ever commit to a relationship
So they call on me
The one who fits the criteria
And set up a quick place to meet
It's not typical
But, I've met in
Hotels, Motels, City Parks, back seats of their cars
Shoot, I've even did one
In the men's bathroom
Right next to the apartment's swimming pool
You know...
Any place will do
You probably saying
"Why is she enjoying such negative attention?"
So let me mention
That any form is good, when you're not getting any
Then one day while on my stroll
I ran into a lady that had to be about 80 years old

She stared at me as if looking through my soul
And said
"Baby you have traveled down a very long and destructive road
Believe me I know what you're doing
But your body is a temple
Something that you should let no man ruin"
Those words from the wise hit home
And from that day
I danced to the beat of a new song
Respect and love that I have for self-begin to uproar
Over powering the hate and self-pity that was there
I reclaimed my life
Doing away with the things that was hindering me
Now I live so vibrant, sophisticated, and free
Unless we're committed
No man deserves to have me sexually
For no one's going to look out
For my well- being, protect, or even love me (like me)

His Representative

It wasn't hard work getting him
Actually that part was easy
Didn't know if that's what I really wanted
But figured that trying was worth it
(At first that's what I thought)
So we chilling right
And, everything is going right
Then things about him begin to change
Slowly detouring from the path that he was on
There was nothing right about taking a left turn
When I started adding it all up
I still came up with a disturbing sum
No matter how much I added a little
And subtracted a lot
Or divided the good from the bad
Even multiplying it all out
I came to the conclusion that
There were a lot of things about himself that this man left out
You were pretty good at acting
So I'll give you that
But your pretending and faking
Is minor stuff to a real person

So I'll give my durn self a standing ovation
For figuring you out
It was very disturbing
Meeting the real man
After being introduced to your representative
But that's something that I'll get over
You'll never have a true lover
For you don't know how to be a true lover to someone else
And if you keep this up
You'll die a lonely man
Because you'll always be by your damn self

You've Changed

Relationship
Do you know what that mean
I mean…
I show more love to you
Then you actually show to me
I know you're not going to always come out even
When you're dealing
In such a gambling situation
The odds seem to be racked against us
Why must we lack such
Loyalty, honesty, and trust
Why when we talk, I consider it a conversation
But the more I talk, you consider it quite annoying
Saying "you go on and on, you just get to rambling"
Never do you want me to express my feelings
And maybe it's because you have no feelings
When it comes to me
I feel like a stranger in my own house
Your nothing like you use to be
No longer your sweet muffin
And I'm tussling
With the fact that
You walk right by me

Without saying nothing
No doubt you owe me something
Like an explanation
On why you think I'm deserving
Of this treatment that you are giving
Lonely days are getting longer
I'm longing
For the day that things get back to the way
They use to be

What Gave You The Right

This can't be right, and
What possessed him to do me like this
How did I get caught up in his mindless acts of craziness
How come the more I scream no
His ears interpret the word yes
How come while fighting so hard
My body becomes so restless
In the midst of 5 minutes, which seemed like eternity
I began to go numb and begin to day dream
Trying to figure it all out
Reasons of why this is happening
I know I did some selfish things
Attitude far from pleasing
But did that give him the right to violate me
I might not have listened, rebuked and didn't pay attention
Might have been a little promiscuous
Flirt a lot in some of my actions
But did that give him the right to violate me
May have even acted like a fool
Disobeyed and played by my own rules
Slipped up and cussed, a time or two
But who the hell are you
To forcefully have sex with me

Do you know what you have done
Ceased all chances of me trusting anyone
Full of pain, regret, and filth
Can't stand to love or even look at myself
My female parts, well I wish they weren't here
Make them all disappear
So I can release all my fears
Of someone violating me again
Hope your suffering be extremely hard and endless
For me..
God is comforting me through all of this
My ultimate healer, that's who he is
Strengthens me so one day I can tell my story
And be of help to another that shares my story

Love Me, No You Don't

You love me
Try telling me something new
For I'm the same one of 21 years
That gave her heart to you
You love me (hmmm)
But two other women are in love with you
Now that's a math problem
That's far beyond solvable
Count it all
Pain, pain, and more pain
You let your threesome bring such family feud
Do you know how it feels
To have another woman break the news
Said that y'all decided to have two kids
Because I couldn't carry any in my womb
And you know in that area I'm sensitive
So why would you share something so fragile
Y'all must be quite serious
For you to disrespect the bond between us two
But then she took another moment
To make sure I knew about the other woman
Said she can't believe you did this
And she not being quiet any longer
Won't continue to be secretive, it all needs to be out in the open
So now I'm sitting here wondering

What gives her the right to be hurt
She messed with another lady's husband
And now the exact same thing is happening to her
She goes on to tell me about baby number 3
That woman number 3 is carrying
Said she not giving up easily
Until this love triangle is settled
So how can you say you love me
How about telling me something else
Hold up, actually I don't want to hear it
Keep your apologies to yourself
I'm all burned out, not an ounce of energy left
And there's nothing you can say
That'll make me want to stay
After 21 years, not willing to split you three ways
Go take care of your 20's
Try to find happiness and be safe
My tears will be short lived
I'll find another to take your place

What Is This

Incents burning Candles lit
Wine on chill, and I prepared your favorite dish
Praying to God that when you get here
You'll appreciate this
Because lately I've noticed
It's been hard to keep your focus
On me... No hugs, no kisses, no intimacy
Guess I'm trying to figure you out
Without actually finding out
Because I'm scared the news might be devastating
It's been 5 months, 4 days, 3 hours, 2 min's, and 1 second
Since the last time you've touched me
Yet walking around me
As if there's nothing wrong with that
Tell me where they do that at
Don't know of any couple behaving like that
For if I'm not the one doing you
Then that means some other woman is screwing you
I can't wait for you to get here
So we can eat dinner and have a conversation
I need all the answers
To every last one of my questions
And I hope you're willing to listen
Because my eyes been weeping, and
My heart's been heavy
Trying to figure out what is this dark cloud
That's dangling over our marriage

Some Explaining To Do

Why must you treat me so bad
If I'm not what you desires then leave
Free yourself from this web
Of whatever it is
That keeps you so pissed off at me
It's your free will I'm not holding you here
The same way you walked through that door
Is the same way that you can walk back out that door
Let's be clear
It's not what I want, but I also don't want you
Feeling as if you're trapped here
Where did I go wrong I cook good meals
Take durn good care of our kids
Even your kids that isn't my biological kids
Folk don't even know the difference
Because I gave a new definition to step mom
What's yours is mine and what's mine is yours
I wash your clothes; I iron, and then neatly fold them up
Keep a clean house
We have way more than some
Financially dependable
And A- 100 in the bedroom
So I need to know where this "fuck off" attitude comes from
You better hurry up and get to explaining
While taking self- inventory and see what needs changing
Or one day you'll look up And I'll be gone

It's Late In The Evening

It's late in the evening
But to me it feels like 5 O'clock in the morning
Because the darkest hour is just before day
So if I make it through this hurting hour
When day break, then everything should be okay
But again it's late in the evening
So I have to face this situation that's right here in my face
One more hour to fight through, before I hit the break of day
Who do I run to
Where do I go
The walls are closing in on each side
Fingers going numb for trying to push them all back
With everything I have in me, on the inside
I'm claustrophobic
I can't ignore it
The pain is written all over my face
It's an emotion that I can't hide
How can something so simple
Be so confusing that it makes me cry
Some say love is simple
It's hurting, it's damaging, and its sadness
It's gone with the wind, peace in my madness
It's joy, its happiness
It's the sunshine in my rain
It's my "No pain then no gain"
Why does one word have so many descriptions

Who do love bring out
So many mixed emotions and feelings
It's late in the evening
And I'm sitting here thinking
That love is not discrimination
Against race, color, sex, or age
If you can't get one your own age or older
To treat you right, what makes you think a younger one
Would do the same
I'm getting older
I can't handle the "tag, your it" game
Not up for no hide and seek
Your steady hiding and creeping
Out here cheating and seeking
A younger version
I'm searching and prying
Came across it and now I'm dying
Praying and hoping
That he's still satisfied with me
His older woman
Now I'm wondering
Got my mind roaming
Losing the love that I thought I've found
It's late in the evening y'all
Why was I out here looking
This late...
For love on this children's playground

Just Being Me

Just being me
Is all I know how to be
Nothing like you
But just like you
When I'm cut I bleed
When hurt my heart weeps
When glad I feel a wonderful glee
I wrote this book to tell my stories
Because although my outside look complete
My insides were filled partially
As if there was always something missing
So don't judge me for continually searching
For we've all encountered
"EXPERIENCES WITH LOVE"
Rather it makes you or breaks you
Never let it completely destroy you
I've come across more bad then good in the end
But I still live to love again

EXPERIENCES WITH LOVE

We all have, Let's continue to love and support one another, without God's love my heart can no longer beat. I love and lost, love and gained and now I love all of you who will pick up this book and read these poem that are from my heart remember I love you even though so of us might never meet personally I love you . INFINITY TIMES INFINITY!! This is form my heart to yours

EXPERIENCES WITH LOVE

I HAVE YOU HAVE WE ALL HAVE !!!!!!!

THE END

ARNIKIA ROBINSON

www.ingramcontent.com/pod-product-compliance
Lightning Source LLC
Chambersburg PA
CBHW071143090426
42736CB00012B/2205